RECOVERING THE LOST SELF

A Liturgical Press Book

RECOVERING THE LOST SELF

Shame-Healing
for Victims of Clergy Sexual Abuse

Elisabeth A. Horst

Published
in association with the
Interfaith Sexual Trauma Institute
Collegeville, Minnesota

THE LITURGICAL PRESS
Collegeville, Minnesota

Designed by Frank Kacmarcik, OBL.S.B.

Library of Congress Cataloging-in-Publication Data

Horst, Elisabeth A.
    Recovering the lost self : shame-healing for victims of clergy sexual abuse / Elisabeth A. Horst.
        p.   cm.
    ISBN 0-8146-2442-1 (alk. paper)
    1. Shame—Religious aspects—Christianity.   2. Sexual abuse victims—Rehabilitation.   3. Sexual misconduct by clergy.
    4. Reconciliation—Religious aspects—Christianity.   I. Title.
    BT714.H67   1998   97-44857
    261.8'32—dc21   CIP

For Diane Dovenberg,
who told me to write page 2

Many thanks for the encouragement, insight, and generosity of those who read the manuscript: Roman Paur, William Doherty, Stephen Rossetti, and Julie Williams.

CONTENTS

FOREWORD

We welcome this volume that is sponsored by the Interfaith Sexual Trauma Institute. The Institute was created in May 1994 by St. John's Abbey and University in partnership with the ISTI Board to address issues within ministry of sexual abuse, exploitation, and harassment through research, education, and publication. The vision of ISTI is the building of healthy, safe, and trustworthy communities of faith.

In its statement of purpose for the Institute, the ISTI Board, with membership from some fifteen Jewish and Christian traditions, strongly affirms the goodness of human sexuality and advocates respectful relationship through the appropriate use of power within communities of all religious traditions. Everyone stands to gain by examining openly together whatever we discover are the issues and by providing the means to confidently promote an informed awareness of our common failure. We must look critically at history, sexuality, human relationships, and our collective struggle to develop sexual meaning.

ISTI believes that human sexuality is sacred; misuse of power underlies all forms of sexual compromise, compromise that violates human dignity and harms individuals and communities both emotionally and spiritually. Healing and restoration are possible for survivors, offenders, and their communities through a complex and painful process. However, truth telling and justice making are integral to change and healing in individuals and institutions.

THE GOALS OF ISTI ARE TO

1 encourage understanding of sexual misconduct through interdisciplinary seminars, conferences, and seminary instruction;

2 develop models of intervention, psychological and spiritual healing, restitution, and recovery of community trust in collaboration with such persons as victims, offenders, religious leaders, and those in the helping professions;

3 support the systematic study of and theological reflection on healthy human sexuality and appropriate use of power;

4 publish materials regarding victims and healing, offenders and rehabilitation, and spiritual communities and their transformation;

5 advance research on sexual abuse, exploitation, harassment, and their prevention;

6 collect and disseminate accurate information about issues of sexual misconduct;

7 network with other professional organizations and agencies that deal with issues of sexual misconduct.

We welcome suggestions. For information on treatment programs, newsletters, workshops and seminars, and other resources for victims and offenders, contact:

Interfaith Sexual Trauma Institute (ISTI)
St. John's Abbey and University Collegeville, MN 56321

Phone: 320-363-3994 Fax: 320-363-3954

E-mail: isti@csbsju.edu
Internet: http://www.osb.org/isti/

Recovering the Lost Self

1

VICTIMS AND SHAME

Sexual abuse victims can feel like lost children. When the abuser is a member of the clergy, the victim may feel lost in relation to God as well as within the human community of the Church. Victims may feel vulnerable and in need of help, painfully aware of their own invisibility, especially to those in authority; and at the same time, they may feel quite reluctant to call attention to themselves, and not altogether sure they want or can use help at all. Many victims feel both urgency and terrible dread at the prospect of the abuse coming to light. They want terribly for someone to know and at the same time dread being found out. Mostly they wish the bad feelings could just go away.

At the center of this internal drama is shame. This booklet is about how victims of sexual abuse perpetrated by clergy can heal from the shame that goes with that abuse.

CLERGY SEXUAL ABUSE

Shame is one of the ongoing, invisible but devastating consequences of clergy sexual abuse. Sexual abuse is the misuse of what is normally a healthy, joyful, and even fun human activity. At its best, human sexuality not only gives great pleasure but also reflects the goodness of creation, deepens love and connection between partners, and increases self-knowledge and understanding of another. But in order for any of this to be possible, sexual activity of any kind must at the very least be consensual.

SEXUAL ABUSE

1 includes inappropriate sexual activity of any kind:
    same-sex or other-sex
    adult-adult or adult-child
    physical or verbal
    violent or nonviolent
2 involves the exploitation of power by the abuser
3 happens when one person does not consent fully
    to sexual activity because of
    use of force by abuser
    use of overt or subtle coercion by person
    of greater power
    limited power to say no on the part of the victim
4 creates additional problems for the victim
    when perpetrated by clergy

Sexual abuse happens when sexual contact is not consensual, either because it is physically forced by one person on another or because the difference in power between those involved is such that someone has limited power to say no. It can be more difficult to say no when your pastor comes on to you sexually than when someone you happen to meet at a party does because the moral authority and leadership status of an ordained person make us more likely to trust that person and to go along with his or her wishes. Clergy have a responsibility to use their power for the good of those they serve, and to take care not to exploit it to meet their own needs at the expense of others. Unfortunately, some clergy misuse their power by engaging in sexual contact that is harmful to others.

Recovering the Lost Self

Sexual misconduct in communities of faith doesn't always, and perhaps doesn't usually, look like the old stereotype of the armed rapist forcing the ambushed victim to submit. It is more likely to involve exploitation of a relationship that already exists, and it may even start off as a positive connection. It may take the form of an initially friendly adult luring children into sexual activities they don't really understand. It may involve a minister having sex in his office with someone who came to him for pastoral care. It may consist of a priest constantly making sexually oriented jokes in the church office or carrying on graphic conversations about sexual topics during visits with members of the congregation.

The effects on victims vary widely. Depending on the type of misconduct and the victim's own history, some victims will experience more emotional trauma than others. One will seek out new and more challenging responsibilities at work, while another will begin having panic attacks so debilitating that she decides to quit. One will feel offended and dirty, another will tell himself the incident didn't mean much. But whatever the level of offense, whatever the material effects on the lives of those involved, inappropriate sexual activity of any kind will create shame in its victims. Healing shame is the foundation of healing from sexual abuse.

SHAME

Shame is a normal human emotion, something everyone experiences from time to time. Without shame we would have a hard time restraining our own risky or inappropriate behaviors. Shame, in fact, is one of the internal restraints that prompt most of us not to act on every sexual impulse

Victims and Shame

we feel. Shame has its own usefulness in human life, just like Tabasco sauce has its own usefulness in cooking.

Any human emotion experienced beyond its range of usefulness and out of proportion to other emotions will shape character and can eventually debilitate a personality. Anger over time becomes chronic bitterness. Normal fear, exaggerated, becomes suspicion, mistrust, and hostile withdrawal. Even pleasure, sought after relentlessly and without regard to other important things in life, becomes hollow hedonism. Shame, when it becomes chronic, loses its usefulness and becomes the crippling habit of self-attack. Shame can prevent victims from seeking help, keep them locked in behaviors that make them vulnerable to further victimization, interfere with intimacy and trust, make it difficult for them to speak up. Shame limits other emotions, and experienced too much for too long it can severely limit one's life.

SHAME
1 normal, universal human emotion
2 feeling of painful self-awareness
3 interrupts other, positive, feelings
4 linked to particular thoughts, feelings, needs, events in each individual
5 can become chronic self-loathing
6 can severely limit activity, creativity, intimacy
7 produced and reinforced by sexual abuse

What is shame? At its most basic, shame is a feeling that interrupts other, positive feelings, and in doing so it produces a global, negative evaluation of the self. Shame is the internal voice that hisses, "Stop that! You're bad!" In subjective experience shame is the sure and certain knowledge that you are completely flawed, defective to the core, deserving of nothing except to disappear. The badness is not so much about anything particular you did, although something you did may have triggered the feeling. It includes all of you, your whole self. In shame you are painfully aware of yourself and therefore exquisitely aware of others' awareness of you. When you experience shame, you want nothing so much as to hide from the judging eyes of others. But solitude in itself does not really bring relief from those accusing eyes, since you can feel them anyway. You know beyond doubt that you would disgust anyone who could see you.

Shame is what makes you stammer, reaching for words you can't locate, when the teacher asks a question you're afraid you can't answer. Shame is the ink that stains your soul black when you open the overdraft notice from your bank. Shame is the powerful physical urge to run from the room when you see yourself on the video of your mother's birthday party. It is the mocking echo inside your head of your own voice, speaking too loudly in the last staff meeting. It is the invisible hand that keeps your head down and your eyes scanning the pattern on the rug when you say something personal. When you feel ashamed, you call yourself names you haven't used to someone else's face since you were eleven years old: stupid, ugly, idiot, sick, crazy, fool, slob, dumb, show-off. Shame feels somehow contagious, as if you will pollute anyone else who sees or touches you.

Shame produces such intense pain that we tend to do whatever we can to stop feeling it and to keep from ever having to feel it again. Sometimes this urge pushes victims to avoid dealing with the shame of the abuse, to go on as if nothing happened, or to bury it under overwork or continuous rage or helping everyone but oneself. Sometimes, however, the urge to get rid of shame can push a victim into healing, dealing openly with the abuse and its effects, deciding intentionally to tend the wounds.

Trauma follows a person through life. It breaks down trust and self-esteem. It punches a hole in the soul.*

Compassionately tended, the wounds of shame do heal over time. Chronic shame does not have to go on forever, and it does not have to rule the lives of victims. Sexual abuse is a set of behaviors, not the essence of a person; it cannot make a victim permanently and completely bad. A victim can choose to grow beyond the narrow limits enforced by shame, to develop a self stronger than the attacks of self-loathing launched against it.

There is a story told of a woman who bravely claimed her own healing from a shameful disease. This story offers a model for others who seek relief from shame. Every victim will follow a different path to healing, and no story has all the answers. Still, guideposts in the form of the experience of others who have gone before can add to one's store of wisdom. This is a story that can become a companion on a healing journey.

THE WOMAN WITH THE HEMORRHAGE

Now there was a woman who had been suffering from hemorrhages for twelve years. She had endured much under many physicians, and had spent all that she had; and she was no better, but rather grew worse. She had heard about

*Quotations are adapted from statements made by participants in the ISTI Discovery Conferences of the Interfaith Sexual Trauma Institute (ISTI).

Jesus, and came up behind him in the crowd, and touched his cloak, for she said, "If I but touch his clothes, I will be made well." Immediately her hemorrhage stopped; and she felt in her body that she was healed of her disease. Immediately aware that power had gone forth from him, Jesus turned about in the crowd, and said, "Who touched my clothes?" and his disciples said to him, "You see the crowd pressing in on you; how can you say, 'Who touched me?'" He looked all around to see who had done it. But the woman, knowing what had happened to her, came in fear and trembling, fell down before him, and told him the whole truth. He said to her, "Daughter, your faith has made you well; go in peace, and be healed of your disease" (Mark 5:25-34).

2

STEPS TO HEALING

She is not even identified by name, but the woman in this story accomplishes for herself what none of the experts have been able to do for her. As we look closely at her story, we see a bold and yet humble woman, someone who has lived in a legal state of shame for a long time, take action on her own behalf, withstand a public challenge to what she has done, and finally find blessing for the miracle that she herself initiated. Victims of sexual abuse in communities of faith can initiate their own healing from shame, as this brave woman did. The steps of the woman's journey include:

1 understanding the state of shame in which she lives
2 seeing that conventional means to healing are not working
3 seeking healing by the means that she herself finds authentic
4 withstanding further shame, and
5 finding witness and blessing for her healing.

Every healing journey is different, and there is no single map that can provide a direct and linear route through shame. Healing takes time, sometimes years, and the traveler will encounter many false starts, numerous switchbacks, unavoidable rest stops, and even once in a while a miraculous leap forward. Journeying from a life ruled by shame to a life in which shame stays mostly within its limits of usefulness is like moving from one town to another. The victim's journey is neither as quick and direct as the car driving along the freeway, nor as aimless and passive as the tumbleweed blowing along at the side of the road. It's a walk that requires patience, stamina, and hope. Many victims will find that the steps taken by the woman in the story provide helpful guideposts along the way.

HEALING SHAME: IF YOU ARE A VICTIM

1 Identify and learn to recognize shame in your life.
   Naming it is the first step. You don't have to spend your life feeling awful and not knowing why.
2 Get out of shame-producing situations.
   This means ending the abuse if it is still going on. No one deserves to stay in an abusive relationship.
3 Take responsibility for your own healing.
   The abuse is not your fault. Recovery is your responsibility.
4 Act as if you have a right to be here.
   Hold your head up. State an opinion. Stop letting shame limit your every move.
5 Seek genuine help and support.
   Find at least one person who believes your story. Make a list of people you can call when things get bad.

3

LIVING IN A STATE OF SHAME

The woman in the story has lived in a state of shame for twelve years. Not only is she suffering a messy and uncomfortable disease, she is, according to Hebrew law, ritually unclean. The law states (Lev 15) that a woman with any sort of uterine bleeding is unclean, and her impurity extends to anything on which she sits or lies down. Anyone who touches her or the things she touches becomes unclean as well and must go through ritual purification. This woman whose bleeding has not stopped for twelve years has been at legal risk of tainting anyone she touches for that entire time. The law has required her to live as an untouchable, in a permanent state of shame. She has been forced to withdraw from human touch, to refuse to give or receive comfort, love, support in any physical way, lest she spread her own pollution to someone else. And all this because of something that has happened to her beyond her control, something she cannot either start or stop.

This situation is in many ways like the state of shame in which those who have been sexually abused within communities of faith live today. Sexual abuse is defined as abusive precisely because one of the participants, the one being abused, has little or no voice. Sexual contact between people of unequal status and power is always suspect because it is impossible for the person of lesser power to give appropriate consent. Like the woman's hemorrhage, sexual abuse is by definition something that happens to the victim outside her or his control. And the shame produced by the abuse often leads victims to feel untouchable, polluted, tainted. Victims speak of themselves as dirty, damaged goods, disgusting. They feel desperately in need of love and support and yet terribly afraid to reach out for it.

SHAME RELATED TO EXTERNAL STANDARDS

There may in fact be a reality base for their fear of reaching out. Many Churches have historically been strong in their teachings about sexual morality. Most religious systems have at times focused on sexuality as an area of life in need of strict regulation. Unfortunately, in such an atmosphere it can be easy for church members to judge any inappropriate sexual activity harshly. In many cases of sexual abuse by clergy it is the victim who has taken the brunt of the community's blame.

Survivors feel responsible. "A priest wouldn't do that, a minister wouldn't do that, a pastoral counselor wouldn't do that; the Church will fall apart if I tell."

This means that the victim is correct to assume, ahead of time, that she or he would be seen as not living up to the moral standards of the community were the abuse discovered. Not only does this in itself create shame, but the resulting secrecy feeds it. Add to this the abuser's perspective, often directly spoken but in any case clearly communicated, that the victim wants or deserves or willingly participates in the abuse. Other members of the community, including the victim, will tend to give more credence to the abuser's perspective because of the position of moral authority held by the clergy. Victims themselves tend to overestimate the degree of their own consent and underestimate the degree of coercion involved. Victims are rarely so helpless as to have absolutely no voice, but partial participation is not the same thing as freely given consent. Victims feel shame because they feel responsible for inappropriate sexual behavior that is by definition not their fault.

SHAME FROM THE ABUSE ITSELF

But victims do not feel shame only because they are aware that their behavior violates community standards. Sexual abuse is in and of itself an inherently shaming activity. Any time one person treats another as an extension of the self, as a thing to be used to gratify needs rather than as a self-directed, separate self with its own needs and interests, the user shames the one used. Sexual abuse is a primary example of a shaming interaction, since the abuser meets his or her own needs at the expense of the needs of the victim. The actions of the abuser in effect say to the victim, "You deserve to be treated like something less than human." It is poignantly easy for a victim to accept and internalize this terrible message. Sexual abuse will reinforce whatever old shame the victim carries, and will also create new shame to add to the burden.

One pastor convinced himself that the chair of the education committee wanted to have sex with him, that she in fact appreciated his sexual advances. She had confided that she suffered from poor self-esteem, particularly related to her belief that she wasn't attractive to men. Telling himself that he was helping her feel better about herself was actually a thin veneer over the pastor's own need to prove to himself that he was attractive to women. Not only did the affair fail to improve anyone's self-esteem, it left the woman feeling more ashamed and unworthy than ever. Since she was being used to shore up the pastor's own shaky self-esteem, she left each sexual encounter feeling a little less prized for herself and her own qualities. As long as the pastor treated her as a means to an end, he increased her store of shame.

SHAME IN THE LIVES OF VICTIMS
Shame acts like a mouse that comes into the pantry only when you're not there. It's easier to recognize it by its effects than to figure out exactly what it looks like and how it gets in. Even when the shame experienced by the victim comes directly from the sexual misconduct, its negative effects spread outward into aspects of life unrelated to the original events. Victims experience shame as global negative self-evaluation: not, "I did a bad thing," but, "I am bad to the core." They may feel that whatever bad things happen to them are their own fault, that they are so wicked God couldn't possibly forgive them, that they are deeply flawed and likely to contaminate others, that their essential unworthiness is obvious to anyone who looks at them. The bad feelings go so far and so deep that it's hard to identify their source. All victims experience the effects of shame in their lives, but many do not connect their shame to the sexual abuse.

In fact, living in a state of shame may not even mean consciously experiencing frequent bouts of shame as a discrete emotion. Shame is so painful that we tend to defend ourselves against it psychologically, substituting excessive blame for ourselves or others, withdrawal from situations where we might feel shame, denial of our own or others' perceptions of the world. Our defenses may be so effective that we almost never feel shame consciously, but instead live lives shaped by avoiding it. Consciously, then, victims of sexual abuse in communities of faith may experience a mixture of feelings related to the abuse itself.

"The abuse is hateful." Some victims experience the abuse as unwelcome, unpleasant, and icky. They may feel confused, particularly about who is responsible, and may feel pressured to act as if they enjoy it. They may in fact outwardly go along so as not to embarrass or risk the retaliation of the abuser, but they experience the events themselves as uncomfortable and disturbing. A group of teenage boys who were often invited to a priest's weekend home knew that the "cost" of the attention, the alcohol, and the pornography the priest provided for them would be that someone had to submit to sexual activity with him. These victims knew they did not like the sexual activity and tried to avoid it.

Victims feel that they must have been really bad, since this holy, God-like person singled them out for the abuse.

Victims who know they hate the abuse at the time report feeling singled out in a negative way. They wonder if they are responsible for sending out "vibes" of availability to potential abusers. "I must be wearing a sign with a big target that says, 'Abuse me,'" said one. These victims may also feel confused by their own participation in activities they know they do not enjoy and blame themselves for not saying no when they know they should. Although they do not like it, they may feel that they somehow deserve the abuse and would deserve punishment if it came to light. The theme of this kind of shame is that one is uniquely bad, dirty, ugly, damaged. These victims tend to hate the offender, and hate themselves as well.

"It's not abuse, it's an affair." Some victims, in contrast, subjectively experience sexual contact with a church leader more as a thrilling affair than as exploitation or abuse. Far from seeking to avoid or ward off the sexual advances of the person with greater power, these victims may believe that they welcome the attention. As adults, we like to believe that we are in control of our actions, and, to a certain extent, we are. An adult woman who seeks counseling from her minister and finds herself sexually involved with him does have more resources available, more personal authority to say yes or no, than a four-year-old who is molested by her Sunday school teacher. This makes it even harder for the woman to understand the ways in which her choices are limited by the authority and status of the minister. Furthermore, if the minister in question is a skillful emotional manipulator rather than an emotional thug, he is likely to try to convince the woman, and himself, that she really does want his sexual advances. He may try to make her feel special, loved, cherished, flattered. She may enjoy the attention and the physical contact and believe that the relationship would be ideal if only it could be carried on openly. She may even be excited by the secrecy. She will often be very concerned about the effects of the sexual activity on the abuser and blame herself for "tempting" him or for posing a threat to his reputation and his standing in the community. Although it is of great importance in these cases to recognize the greater power of the clergy person or church leader, and to hold him or her accountable for

violation of boundaries, it is also important to acknowledge that in these cases the victim may not identify herself as a victim at all. These victims may be conscious of shame related to violating others' standards, particularly if the sexual contact is discovered, but may not be aware of feeling shame directly related to the behavior itself.

When you are abused in a church setting, you miss experiencing the unconditional love of God.

This is not to say, however, that shame does not impact the lives of these apparently consenting victims. Any relationship founded in the exploitation of power will produce shame, whether or not the participants are aware of it at the time. In a case like this the shame will tend to surface as if it were related to other areas of the victim's life. These victims will experience moments of feeling worthless, stupid, incompetent, bad, of wanting to disappear, of believing they can do nothing right or have no right to speak up for themselves. One may say, "Everything in my life is going well except my job," or another, "Nothing in my life is going well except this relationship." Consciously the victim experiences these feelings as relating to work, parenting, school, friendships, body image, anything but "the affair." Outside her awareness, the experience of being exploited is reinforcing her belief that she deserves to be used.

"I'm not sure how I feel." A third group of victims will have a very hard time identifying any feelings at all about the abuse. Often these victims express confusion at their own lack of feeling. They know they should be able to feel something. They think perhaps they ought to feel bad about

what's happened to them, but it just doesn't seem to bother them or to affect their lives much. These victims may feel emotionally numb and detached in many areas of their lives and may feel vaguely disturbed that they seem to function "like a robot" at work and at home.

Like other emotions, shame will not be a large part of the conscious experience of these individuals. Typically, though, they will adopt a self-deprecating style, saying frequently how they are never doing enough, never good enough, too lazy or stupid or ugly to deserve approval. The numbness in which these victims live by and large protects them from moments of stabbing shame, and it also keeps them behaving as if they are unworthy of forming an identity or will of their own. They may have trouble separating their wishes from someone else's and thus may believe that since the abuser wants the sexual contact the victim wants it as well, or should want it, or shouldn't refuse it. They may forget that the sexual contact happened, or even in some sense convince themselves that it is not really happening, or at least it is not very important. They may develop one set of behaviors and feelings that operate during times of inappropriate sexual contact and an entirely different set that operate at other times.

In cases of sexual abuse by clergy, the truth is severely wounded. There is a lot of denial.

One woman described feeling little distress or awkwardness when she attended a potluck dinner at church and sat at a table with both her husband and the minister with whom she had been sexually involved. She knew other people might be bothered in the same situation, and thought perhaps she ought to feel guilty, but she couldn't find any bad feelings at all.

The real problem with her extreme lack of distress is not that she should be feeling bad about her own behavior. The problem is that she has disconnected herself from her ability to feel pain and injury to herself. Like someone who loses sensation in the palm of the hand following surgery, a victim who loses her ability to feel emotional pain is at terrible risk of being badly harmed before she knows it. She may not feel pain, but she doesn't know to pull away from a hot stove either. Victims who remain unaware of their emotions keep themselves constantly vulnerable to further exploitation.

VISIBLE EFFECTS OF SHAME

All these types of victims live lives deeply influenced by shame. Whether suffered acutely or avoided completely, shame can act like an electric fence that keeps a person in familiar but limited territory. Shame can prevent healthy intimacy, feed addictions, prompt self-injurious or self-defeating behavior. One victim spent seventeen years in a job she hated, hadn't wanted in the first place, but felt she couldn't say no to when asked. She felt so ashamed at the thought of admitting that she might want a different job that she just stayed put, until, in therapy, she had begun to examine the sources of her shame. Another went from one sexual relationship to another, constantly ashamed at her sexual behavior, constantly seeking relief from her shame about sexuality in yet another sexual encounter. Another felt ashamed of her loss of faith, and so continued to go to church and sing in the choir, feeling more and more empty with every service, as if God no longer had any interest in her. For each of these victims, the healing process involved careful attention to the specific problem areas—career, sexuality and relationships, spirituality—as well as careful tending to the shame wounds behind the behavior.

4

TRYING TO HEAL USING CONVENTIONAL METHODS

Victims do not live lives limited by shame because they want to, or because they like it that way, or because they are masochists. People stay in shame because it seems like the best choice at the time. Most sexual abuse victims try hard to make themselves feel better, even if they only vaguely sense that something is wrong.

Most people start out trying to solve the problem of the shame they feel by using what I would call conventional methods—the common-sense wisdom recommended by parents, peers, and by the faith communities to which they belong. Where better to seek healing for feelings of deep unworthiness than in one's spiritual home or through the wisdom of one's elders?

The pastor said, "Go home and pray about the abuse." And she came back having prayed, and nothing had changed. He said, "You just didn't pray hard enough, and that's your fault."

Sometimes these conventional, familiar resources do indeed help to reduce shame. Sometimes, though, they do not. By the time the woman with the hemorrhage sought out Jesus, she had tried the conventional route to healing her disease. Not only had she spent all her money, she was getting worse instead of better. Whatever remedies the physicians had to offer simply did not work; nor did the law that required that she refrain from touching anyone. The standard advice increased her distress rather than reducing it. Somewhere along the way she concluded that it was time to try something completely different instead of going back for more of the same.

What constitutes a healing path versus an unhealthy journey into "more of the same"? The answer will vary from one victim to another. The single defining criterion is whether whatever remedy is chosen makes the individual feel more or less ashamed. This can be a tricky thing to observe. Sometimes strategies that produce more shame in the moment lead to gradual healing over time. This is often true of telling one's story to a sympathetic listener. Sometimes activities that temporarily soothe shame will actually increase it over time. Self-destructive or self-injurious behaviors often give immediate relief from feelings that seem intolerable, but in the long run add to the victim's sense of defectiveness. Furthermore, the same words, the same actions, can mean different things and produce different feelings depending on the context and the people involved. Buying a new dress may be a courageous statement of improved self-worth or part of a destructive pattern of attempting to ease emotional pain by over spending. Seeking out a new relationship may create a new source of support or a new source of abuse. The only way to tell the difference is for the victim to develop the unfamiliar habit of analyzing everything in terms of her own self-interest. This requires reconnecting with one's ability to sense danger, learning to trust one's own opinions, learning to evaluate on the basis of how something feels from one's own point of view rather than how it looks from someone else's. To someone who has been treated as if others' needs matter more than her own, this is a challenging task.

Many things that turn out to be more of the same are those things we use to numb feelings. Alcohol and drugs obviously belong in this category; so do binge eating and compulsive spending. So, also, do some things that don't get a person into trouble as fast, such as keeping oneself busy all the time, watching television for hours, even reading or cultivating a "positive" (read: fake) attitude. Any of these can become substitutes for facing difficult or unpleasant feelings.

HEALING AND THE COMMUNITY OF FAITH

A church or other community of faith can be the best friend and the worst enemy of a victim of sexual abuse. Often the community in which the abuse took place is both at the same time. This issue is particularly relevant, and particularly poignant, for victims. Most of us bring our deepest needs to our faith communities, and most religious institutions hold out the promise of a better life when we live according to their teachings and within their fellowship. The fact that sexual misconduct happens within faith communities is one indication that this promise does not always hold true. Only the individual victim can finally decide whether she will be able to find healing from the shame caused by abuse within the particular community or even the particular faith tradition in which it occurred. Because of the religious authority of the abuser, many victims of clergy sexual abuse feel alienated not only from their Church but from God as well.

Traditional religious practices can unintentionally reinforce victims' shame. Someone who lives in constant shame will likely understand religious language and teaching differently from someone who does not. It is very important to understand that the same words will take on different meanings to different people at different times. Many Christian Churches, for instance, include confession of sin as a regular element of worship or spiritual practice. Repeating the words of confession may allow a particular person to feel forgiven, to experience herself as a worthy and cherished child of God, to empower herself to start life anew, to reshape her life in the knowledge that she is not permanently tainted, that God's forgiveness is greater than anything she might have done wrong. The person sitting next to her in the pew may instead experience the practice of confession as an opportunity to call up and sit in her own shame. Repeating the very same words, this person will end the prayer feeling more aware of her unworthiness, more conscious of her faults and failings, more convinced that she can do no better no matter how hard she tries. She may even add an extra twist and tell herself how bad she is for not being able to experience the forgiveness that confession is supposed to produce. Everything is her own fault and she must never forget it.

So the same prayer of confession can help to heal shame or severely reinforce it. It is treacherously easy for clergy, and others responsible for public services, to dismiss the victim's point of view by trying to explain it away. Church leaders need to resist the temptation to say that the person who experiences confession as a form of shame induction is "just praying wrong." Telling a victim that she needs to change in order to be able to understand the intent of the prayer as written is just another subtle way to shame her. A non-shaming alternative is to assume that the victim is praying right. That is, she is praying the words with the meanings they have for her. She is bringing her own experience of being shamed to the words and is therefore perceiving accurately the meaning that those words hold in her life. The way out of the problem is to change the words, not the one praying the words. One victim's spiritual experience changed dramatically when she wrote her own prayer of affirmation and used it in the place of confession. When victims become collaborators in creating religious services and rituals, they can create opportunities for healing shame.

One strategy for healing is the use of worship as the celebration of the healing process.

It can help victims to know that not all churches are the same. Even within the same Christian denomination, different congregations will vary as to the amount of emphasis on shame-related language used in services and among the members. Preaching and teaching that stress the importance of self-sacrifice, personal repentance, and unconditional forgiveness of others may have their place. To a victim who believes the abuse was all her fault anyway, and who is afraid to speak up for fear of hurting the abuser, this kind of emphasis can sound like advice to stay stuck in shame and fear. There is no reason not to seek diligently for a spiritual home that helps to heal shame rather than adding to the burden.

5

SEEKING AUTHENTIC HEALING

What do you do when you've realized that everything you've already tried to get rid of your shame hasn't worked? When you can tell you're feeling worse and not better? You can either drive in that same rut a while longer, or you can turn the steering wheel and head toward whatever it is you know you really need.

ACTION STEPS TO HEALING SHAME

1 Act on your own behalf.
2 Develop a healthy sense of self.
3 Talk to someone you can trust.
4 Find a healthy, affirming spirituality.
5 Speak your truth.
6 Withstand the backlash that follows change.
7 Develop and rely on good interpersonal support.

As the action of the story begins, the woman has realized that she can accomplish the healing of the disease that defines her as untouchable only by reaching out herself to touch someone with the gift of healing. She knows she is breaking the rules, and she expects her actions will be unwelcome. This is why she tries to split the difference, to touch only something that touches Jesus, not to touch the man himself. She is not greedy; she is willing to take the least possible effective amount of healing touch. She does not want to offend, and she does not want to trouble anyone.

But she does want to heal, and she is ready and able at last to risk doing what she herself knows will accomplish that end. No longer willing to trust the letter of the law, no longer willing to obey the word of the experts who tell her what is best, she goes out to steal her own healing. And as soon as she willfully and intentionally ends her years of shunning human contact, she feels her bleeding stop.

One thing we can all do is keep talking about this problem, because if the church leaders are not going to do anything about the abuse that goes on, then it is our responsibility to do something.

ACT ON YOUR OWN BEHALF

Any time a victim takes action on her own behalf, she is healing a bit of her shame. Any time a victim acts as if she has the right to be whole and happy, she is undoing a piece of her self-loathing. Any time he decides not to live within the rules that maintain his state of shame, he is moving forward to his own healing.

The bold action required in a particular victim's life may be as simple as carrying on a ten-minute conversation in which she never once apologizes for herself. It may be as risky as saying no to further abuse. It may mean sitting comfortably rather than in the posture that takes up the least amount of space. It may mean telling the boss or one's mother what's really going on instead of what they want to hear. It may mean forming a real opinion about something and saying it out loud. It may mean taking responsibility for something she did wrong without letting herself sink into feeling like a bad person. The most important thing is that the healing action be consistent with the victim's own understanding of what she or he needs. Healing from shame must be grounded in the authentic selfhood of the individual. Any rules and guidelines and wisdom that come from external sources must be adapted and interpreted to fit the particular needs of the victim, not the other way around.

But how does a victim go about finding her own path to healing? How did the woman know that touching Jesus would be the cure for her? It's one thing to realize that whatever you have been trying hasn't worked, and another thing entirely to figure out what to try next.

In *Women Who Run with the Wolves,* Clarissa Pinkola Estes calls the aspect of self we must consult under these circumstances the inner wise woman. No matter how badly a victim has been hurt, she has her own supply of wisdom and clear-sightedness. True, people who are deeply ashamed will at times make poor choices. But this does not mean that victims are stupid or self-defeating or incapable, or that they ought to let someone else make their decisions for them. The task is to find and strengthen the victim's own ability to discriminate and decide. Figuring out how to use one's own wisdom and will on one's own behalf may be one of the more confusing and difficult steps in the healing process. Still, if he pays attention, a victim really can notice when he feels more ashamed, and when he feels better about himself. He can identify people with whom he feels safe. He can see how some things he does reduce his shame and some things open him up to more bad feelings. He can imagine a day in which he doesn't feel or act ashamed.

For most of us, the experience of healing comes not in one dramatic incident but in many small experiences. Many a victim has experienced a significant moment of healing when she told a therapist or a support group about the worst thing that happened to her and still felt accepted. Or when she talked with a pastor or church leader who didn't come on to her, didn't touch her or sexualize her, didn't make up her mind for her, didn't want anything from her. Or found the courage to go outside her community of faith, for a time or for good.

DEVELOPING A HEALTHY SENSE OF SELF

Notice that the woman in the story does not act against others, but for herself. Even though she breaks the law and risks defiling another person in the process, she intends no harm. She is not seeking revenge but simply going after what she knows she needs. We will never know exactly why she waited twelve years to claim her healing, but one possibility is that she was so busy trying not to bother anyone that it took her that long to figure out what she really needed. Maybe she wanted to be a really good patient, so she paid attention to what the physicians wanted from her rather than what she needed from them. Maybe she was focused so completely on the behavior the community expected of her that it never occurred to her to step out of bounds. Touch someone? But that was forbidden. She certainly couldn't risk polluting someone else. It might offend them.

It's hard to know what you need in order to heal if you can only focus clearly on the needs of others. In order to heal shame, a victim must take the unfamiliar, even revolutionary, step of choosing to act solely out of her own interest. It goes against all the old Sunday school notions of "nice" to stop worrying about inconveniencing someone else, to focus on one's own life rather than the interests of the abuser, the spouse, the friends, the parents. Focusing on one's own healing may even mean giving up trying to teach

the abuser to behave better. Holding an abuser publicly accountable for his or her actions can be an act of justice and
a validating experience, but it will not on its own heal the
shame of the victim. Shame is an internal experience, and
transforming it requires a healthy focus on oneself and
one's own needs.

Survivors feel unlovable and unworthy in the sight of God.

What do victims need? Mostly to live life well. If shame is
about not being worthy, not being smart, not being pretty,
not being good, not being sane, or simply not deserving to
be at all, then its greatest antidote is simply to be oneself.
Form an opinion. Make a choice. Cry if you're sad, and
laugh if it's funny. Take up space. If you're not sure which
fork to use at a formal dinner, use your spoon instead, and
then notice that no one kicks you out for being different.
Whenever you find yourself worrying about what someone
else thinks of you, ask yourself instead, what do I think of
that person? If you are sitting in class or a meeting and feel
crowded, move your chair to give yourself more room. Take
the risk of asking someone to do something for you at least
once a week. On the other hand, don't let anyone do something for you that you could just as well do yourself. Admit
to being good at something. Learn to give and receive
genuine compliments, and do not stay in situations or with
people by whom you feel criticized. Find a spiritual home
in which you feel encouraged rather than punished.

TALK TO SOMEONE YOU CAN TRUST
These many small experiences of healing shame usually
have the quality of an encounter, perhaps with oneself, per-

haps with the divine, but most certainly at some point with other flesh and blood humans. Shame feeds on secrecy, silence, invisibility. Somewhere in the healing process the victim will need to talk to someone about the abuse and about the pain. It was not enough for the woman in the story to sit at home and think of Jesus; she had to go out and risk the actual encounter. The single most effective cure for shame is the experience of being seen and understood exactly as you are by someone who has no need or wish for you to be anything different. This means that the most basic form of healing "touch" for shame is compassionate talk.

It matters a great deal whom a victim chooses to talk to. Chances are the victim, in the wisest part of herself, already can recognize when someone seems to understand her point of view, when someone is willing to sit with whatever feelings she has at the moment, when someone seems able to listen to her story without feeling shocked or overwhelmed by it. If she pays attention, she will notice when she is with someone she doesn't need to take care of, worry about, flatter, cajole, or apologize to. If she has had trouble recognizing these things before, it probably wasn't because she wasn't picking up danger signals, but because she overrode her internal alarm system. Abusers often rely on victims to believe their words rather than their actions. If someone cuts your screen, climbs in your window, picks up your portable TV, and says "I'm not a burglar," you already have everything you need to know whether to believe what he says.

It is important to recognize the difference between telling the story to bring about justice and telling the story in a way that will heal shame. A victim may decide (or not) at some point to talk about the abuse with people in the faith community, with church authorities or legal officers, but that is not the primary or the only conversation needed in order to heal her shame. Shame-healing talk is more likely to come in the form of professional help (counseling or psychotherapy), support groups (therapist led or self-help), or conversations with compassionate friends. Its focus is on the victim, the victim's needs, the victim's feelings, not on the abuser.

The Church is not always a safe place for truth telling.

A victim is likely to be safest, particularly in choosing a professional helper, if he tells his story to someone not involved with the abuser in any way, someone outside of the community in which the abuse happened. This way the helper has no need to take sides, no interest in the outcome of the situation except that the victim feels better. Since talk will not have the effect of healing if it leads to further exploitation, the victim also will want to be sure to tell the story to someone he knows will not be sexual with him, someone who will not push him to take actions he does not want to undertake or does not feel ready for, someone who will not tell anyone else about the conversation unless directly asked to. Anyone who reminds the victim right away of the abuser, either in appearance or behavior, may trigger too many feelings associated with the abuse for the victim to be able to tell the story comfortably. A true shame-healing conversation is one in which the victim can look honestly at the sexual abuse with someone who will not blame him for it, someone who does not believe he is tainted for life.

6

BECOMING VISIBLE

We'd like the story to end here, with the woman healed and free to go on about her life, but she has one more challenge to face. In some ways, this one is the worst of all. Healing isn't completed with the first touch, the first experience of being fully oneself. Once the victim figures out what it would mean to stop behaving like someone deeply ashamed and to start acting like a whole person, she has to practice her new behavior out where people can see her. The problem is, allowing oneself to be seen will bring on more shame at first. In some deep place the victim knew that already, or she wouldn't have taken such pains to hide in the first place. You can't heal from shame without learning to handle the backlash that comes from becoming visible.

It's time for victims to break the silence and be honest about who we are and what our pasts have dealt us.

The woman in the story takes what she needs without asking, as if she is doing her very best not to draw attention to herself. But Jesus knows someone touched him, and he doesn't go along with the woman's agenda. He won't let her slip away without owning what she has done. In one of those moments that last only a few seconds but seem, to the woman at least, to go on for hours, he stops in his tracks to ask who touched him. Maybe the woman could have slipped away anyway; certainly she could have denied what she did, or apologized, said it was an accident. Instead she stands her ground and tells the truth. She does so in fear and trembling, to be sure: she understands the degree of her legal offense, and she has reason to fear the reaction of the crowd. Still, she tells the whole story, without falsification or excuse.

So often the reward for taking one step forward in healing shame is the opportunity to confront yet more shame. It's a lot like the time at the committee meeting when you offered to take on the task nobody else wanted to do. The next time they need someone to make eighty-five phone calls, they come straight to you. "You did it so well the last time," they say. "Here." The reward for doing it well is that you get to do it again.

Sometimes it's easier the second time, but when shame is involved, finding oneself facing more shame right away may feel unbearable. Healing shame means risking exposure, and for someone suffering chronic shame exposure is one of the most emotionally painful experiences of all. If anything that can be seen is grounds for criticism, then holding still long enough to be seen will be terrifying. Claiming one's right to live outside the limits of untouchableness and invisibility necessarily involves giving up the safety of those limits as well.

As anyone who has experienced this kind of exposure knows, it's not always Jesus we encounter. There are plenty of folks who will be shocked, offended, angry when a victim tells what happened, and who will direct their negative energy at the victim. These are the people who blame the victim for the abuse, who refuse to believe the victim's story. They say things like, "Why are you making such a fuss about this? Aren't you over this yet? Think of all the innocent people who will suffer if word of this gets out." Or, "Don't you think you were kind of asking for it? Why didn't you just tell him to stop? I just don't see how it could have happened the way you say it did. Why are you trying to blame someone else for something you did?"

Most of the backlash, however, comes from the victim's own internalized shame. Chances are, before a victim speaks up, she could list all the negative reactions she is likely to get, and worse. She carries enough shame inside herself to supply a whole congregation with mean things to say. To be sure, the shame she now carries inside originated outside herself. It came from the experience of being abused and from the widespread tradition of blaming the victim in our culture as well. But even if the person to whom you dare to show your inner self meets your words with compassion and acceptance—and this can happen if you choose carefully whom to talk to—the internal backlash of shame will be at least as bad as anything anyone else could say.

It's when this backlash hits that the victim begins to wonder why she ever spoke up, why she ever decided to try to get better, why she thought things were so bad the way they were. To the victim this is when it feels like the world is falling apart around her, or maybe it's her falling apart while the rest of the world can't even see anything is the matter. This is when she has trouble sleeping, she thinks about starting to drink again, she would do anything to just end this pain if she knew for sure it would work. She needs desperately to talk to someone but is afraid to call and let anyone see her "like this." It seems like a terrible insult and yet a fitting indication of her insignificance that the world can simply go on around her. She wonders if it would help to hide in the corner, or under the table. Or better yet, go out and get hit by a bus. It's hard to believe anyone can survive such intense pain as shame, met undefended, can produce.

So what does a victim do to survive the backlash of shame? All she really has to do is remember to breathe. Shame hurts, but, left to run its course, it also passes. The only trick is to let it. Just continue to be, and do whatever you can to make yourself comfortable until the pain eases. This is hard medicine to take in the midst of a full-blown shame attack. When this kind of pain descends, we naturally want something to make it all go away. In our results-oriented culture, we have been told time and again that fast pain relief is readily available, and we have a right and duty to buy the pills that produce it. In this kind of environment it's terribly hard to accept that the quickest route out of the suffering is actually the most direct route through it. To feel what you feel as you feel it, to know that you are who you are and therefore should be no other way, is a simple concept and a difficult practice. It's a paradox: change, and therefore healing and growth, can only come out of a radical acceptance of oneself exactly as one is.

Something significant happens when a victim stops avoiding shame and turns to face it instead. There are things one learns when one survives the worst the internal defense system can launch back at the self, things that can't be learned any other way. No one would wish to have to face such a painful experience, but once someone has been through it she doesn't have to be afraid of it in the same way again. Only by living through a real shame attack can a victim know that she is more than her shame, more than what anybody else might think of her, more than the negative opinions she holds of herself. Even when she is most ashamed, she is other things as well. One can feel deeply ashamed and still make a cup of coffee, answer the phone, look out the window, write words on paper. One second to the next, one minute to another, she can feel this pain and still live. She can be herself and survive. She can speak and not die of it. As long as she can stay aware, observe herself in the pain, then some tiny fraction of her is not in it. And once she knows this, shame loses some of its power to limit and direct her life. After she has made it through this terrible tunnel of shame, a victim can know that there really is no such thing as deserving to exist. There is simply the fact of existence. And for better or worse, here we are.

7

FINDING WITNESS
AND BLESSING FOR HEALING

In the story it is clear that the woman's faith, her own internal initiative, is the healing agent. Still, it matters that Jesus declares and blesses the healing that she herself accomplished. Here we find another paradox: Only you can heal yourself, but you cannot accomplish your healing alone.

If healing shame is primarily about being, then what do we need others for? No one else can continue to exist for the victim except the victim herself. No one else can do the hard work of deciding what she needs and becoming visible. And yet she can't do her healing all alone in her room. Visibility requires a pair of eyes other than one's own.

Not being heard was the biggest frustration.

We need others to witness our healing. Witnesses come in different varieties. They can be friends or strangers; they can affirm major steps taken or notice a tiny change; they can understand exactly what courage and practice and hard work your new behavior involves, or not have a clue how much it means. One victim told about calling to set up phone service when she opened her own consulting business. "And is this a business line?" the man helping her asked. "Yes," she said, trembling. "He went right on to the next question!" she told a friend later. "He didn't say, 'You? Start a business?'" Of course she realized that the phone company would have little interest in objecting to collecting the higher business rate, but still the willingness of a complete stranger to accept her definition of herself as a business owner boosted her own belief in herself.

Shame is learned interpersonally. We take in information about ourselves based on how we perceive others responding to us. Learning to anticipate others' attacks on our worthiness may not be a happy way to live, but it usually functions to keep us safe at the time. Unlearning the habit of self-attack must initiate within the victim but can only grow and develop in the healing space of safe relationships.

SPOUSE/PARTNER

If the victim is in a committed relationship, support and understanding from the spouse or partner is critical. It is also difficult for many partners to provide. Spouses are often confused and upset as they relate to a victim who is pursuing a healing journey. A partner will naturally wish for things to stay exactly as they are in the relationship, not because he wants the victim to continue to live with pain, but because any change in one partner will require adjustment and change in the other partner. It may help the victim to understand that it is normal for a partner to resist change. But this does not mean the victim should apologize for initiating it. Any partner has the right to renegotiate a relationship, to ask for substantial changes in everything from the way the laundry gets done to the way Thanksgiving is celebrated.

As humans, we have the right to feel sad and angry today even if we were happy yesterday. Anyone at any time has the right to say no to a particular sexual activity, even if she or he has been saying yes for the last ten years. A partner does not have to like all the changes the victim asks for, but if the relationship is going to last, he or she will need to listen and try to understand. An understanding partner can become an ally, a primary witness to healing.

Intimacy is a sense of mutuality, equality, non-competitiveness, the ability to be vulnerable, the opportunity to be truly alive and be oneself without any change needed.

Someone once defined a supportive spouse as one who has no immediate plans for your improvement. A partner who can listen without judging can learn to understand what it means to heal from shame, even if the partner has not been victimized. One man asked the woman he was dating, "Why do you keep going to therapy if you feel so upset when you come out each week? What good does it do to dig up all that old stuff?"

Another man asked his wife, "Aren't you over this yet? You've been going to that group for three months now. Hasn't it helped at all?" It is important that a victim faced with such questions decide for herself how much she is willing to explain and arrive at a clear understanding of the difference between keeping her partner informed and justifying her behavior to him. The woman who had been in the group for three months took a few deep breaths and then said, "Yes, the group is helping me. I do not know exactly how long this process will take, but sometimes getting better means feeling worse for a while. Right now I just need you to let me be sad." The husband still didn't understand completely, but he decided to offer to make tea instead of keeping up the argument. It was a small gesture, but a significant one, since it indicated his willingness to be with her exactly as she was.

SUPPORT GROUPS

A supportive spouse or partner is a blessing, but it is too much to expect one human being to provide all the support necessary in the healing process. Victims often find support groups very helpful. People who have been through similar experiences, felt the same feelings, struggled with the same shame, have an especially powerful type of validation to offer. You don't have to explain everything to someone who has been there too. In a group, a victim can say, "I saw the abuser on the street yesterday," and see heads nod. No one in the room will be surprised when she says she went straight home without finishing her errands. No one will need her to explain why her stomach lurched and her hands shook on the way home. A lot of shame can be healed quickly when a victim tells her story in a safe group and discovers she is neither alone nor crazy. Compassion, empathy, and respect create a context in which a healthy self can grow beyond the narrow limits of shame.

What a victim really wants is to hear people say, "I believe you."

COMMUNITIES OF FAITH

Churches and other faith communities can witness and bless the healing of victims by listening to the stories and affirming what victims themselves are doing to renew their own lives. This does not mean that it is the victim's responsibility to make those in positions of power understand and acknowledge the pain and damage of the abuse. It helps if it happens, but no victim has to postpone her healing until someone in power sees the need to support her process.

HEALTHY SPIRITUALITY FOR VICTIMS

1 may take place inside or outside organized, institutional religion
2 allows the victim to claim and follow her/his own spiritual path
3 must have room for the victim's doubts, fears, and anger at God and the abuser
4 must affirm the victim as whole and good, exactly as he or she is
5 celebrates and supports the healing process

Jesus was not a member of the religious establishment, but an outspoken, flaky, and even dangerous radical. Within her community of faith, the woman with the hemorrhage found practices that entrenched her shame by reinforcing her isolation. She decided to seek out witness and blessing where it was available rather than waiting for the community to come around to helping her. If she can see that her own faith community does not offer witness and blessing appropriate to her needs, a victim may want to seek out one that does. This may mean finding a small group within the larger church of which she is a part, a group that includes people who understand and perhaps even work for change from within the organization. Or it may mean leaving altogether, finding another congregation, another denomination, another faith where she can feel more whole. She may even want to pursue her own spiritual path outside an organized community.

Finding Witness and Blessing for Healing

Many victims have learned to find and develop their spirituality outside the institutional Church, and others have grown angry with God. For all victims, the abuse means a horrific loss of their rootedness and their basic belief system.

8

THE END IS ONLY THE BEGINNING

The story ends at a point of new beginnings. We are left to imagine what the woman's life is like once she is no longer bleeding. We might assume that her life just went back to normal, but what would "normal" be after twelve years of disease?

No one wants to go on living in shame, but many people feel real fear and confusion when they find out it is actually in their power to go forward without it. Like the alcoholic who gives up drinking, a victim can find out that shame, his worst enemy, was also a kind of friend. What can a victim who is becoming a survivor do with all the time he used to spend scrutinizing himself, body and soul, for faults? How will he decide where to go now that he has turned off the current to the invisible electric fence that marks off the territory of forbidden behavior? Freedom is scary. You get to decide what to do with your time, but you have to give up your excuses. Taking responsibility for your actions and opinions means you have no one else to blame if you don't like where they take you. If you follow your secret heart and take up painting, or dancing, or biochemistry, you will have to live with the fact that what you produce may or may not ever achieve genius quality. If a victim gives up her shame, then she is left face to face with herself. That self will be both more whole than the one cramped by her inner critics, and less grand than the one she might have dreamed of in her narrow prison.

Many victims find that as shame heals, relationships change. Friendships, marriages, religious faith, work roles will shift significantly as a victim begins to act like a survivor, no longer restrained by her shame. Some relationships will not withstand the changes, but the ones that do become stronger because of them. When a victim heals from debilitating shame, she has more self to share, more capacity to be present, less time to waste being compliant and nice.

Healing shame does not mean going back to normal. It means going forward into a whole new life. The healing story is exciting, but the most exciting chapter of a victim's life is what comes next. The adventure is about to begin.

FOR FURTHER READING

Bass, E., and L. Davis. *The Courage to Heal: A Guide for Women Survivors of Sexual Abuse.* New York: Harper Collins, 1988.

Fortune, M. *Is Nothing Sacred? When Sex Invades the Pastoral Relationship.* San Francisco: Harper & Row, 1987.

Kaufman, G. *Shame: The Power of Caring.* Cambridge, Mass.: Schenkman Publishing Company, 1985.

Maltz, W. *The Sexual Healing Journey: A Guide for Survivors of Sexual Abuse.* Chicago: Stern's Books, 1991.

Peterson, M. *At Personal Risk: Boundary Violations in Professional-Client Relationships.* New York: W. W. Norton, 1992.

Rossetti, S. *A Tragic Grace: The Catholic Church and Child Sexual Abuse.* Collegeville: The Liturgical Press, 1996.

About the Author:

Elisabeth A. Horst, Ph.D., is a licensed psychologist in private practice in Minneapolis.